And After All

AND
AFTER
ALL

POEMS BY
Rhina P. Espaillat

ABLE MUSE PRESS

Able Muse Press

www.ablemusepress.com

Printed in the United States of America

Library of Congress Control Number: 2018931558

ISBN 978-1-77349-022-9 (paperback)
ISBN 978-1-77349-019-9 (digital)

Cover image: "For Giving" by Alexander Pepple
(with "hand and rose" by Imani Clovis)

Cover & book design by Alexander Pepple

Able Muse Press is an imprint of *Able Muse:* A Review of Poetry, Prose & Art—at
www.ablemuse.com

Able Muse Press
467 Saratoga Avenue #602
San Jose, CA 95129

For Alfred, always

Acknowledgments

I am grateful to the editors of the following journals where many of these poems originally appeared, sometimes in earlier versions:

14 by 14
Alabama Literary Review
Botteghe Oscure
The Chimaera
The Confluencia Anthology
The Connecticut River Review
Crisis
Ecotone
The Evansville Review
First Things
The Formalist
Garden Lane
The Hudson Review
Iambs and Trochees
Ibbetson Street
The Jewish Women's Literary Annual
Landscapes with Women
Light
Literary Matters

Literature and Arts of the Americas
Lucid Rhythms
Margie
Measure
Mezzo Cammin
Not Just Air
Oberon
Orphic Lute
Per Contra
The Powow River Anthology
Presence
The Raintown Review
Rattle
Scribble
The Sewanee Theological Review
Spindrifter
Think
Voices International

I am grateful, also, to the Powow River Poets, for their encouragement and invaluable critical advice.

Contents

Oh, Wow!

The Bargain

And After All

Things That Go

Links

In this lost moment that the lens once caught,
my son turns, bending slightly, toward his son
as if to hear more clearly what is not
spoken in words at all. Look how each one—
the quiet man in blue and the small boy
in his red shirt, attentive and aware—
is equally at rest, held by the joy
of one another's presence, how the air
between them shines with it, as with a glow
more lasting than mere day. The child has grown
tall as his father now, who years ago
outgrew a father who outgrew his own:
an endless chain whose links cannot endure.
But this caught moment says it holds secure.

Ephemera

My father's garden housed a tank that held
the varicolored silk of tropic rain
we drew out of the rusty spigot, skein
after skein unspooling. And it smelled,

once settled in the pitcher's shallow pool,
fungal and summer-leafy, faintly rank,
so that each sense intuited the tank,
inside, was dark and slippery and cool.

I liked finding ephemera that coiled
and uncoiled in it, every twisting dot
a crystal clown—some harmless, and some not.
The water lost its tang when it was boiled,

and its malarial poison; fit for drinking,
cooled in the earthen vessel where we poured
mere water, to be dipped for with a gourd.
Now, decades hence, decanting it by thinking,

I taste it in a dream, thirsty again,
with memory so tainted by desire
I can forgive the chill paludic fire
and almost think water was sweeter then.

Butchering

My mother's mother, toughened by the farm,
hardened by infant's burials, used a knife
and swung an axe as if her woman's arm
wielded a man's hard will. Inured to life
and death alike, "What ails you now?" she'd say
ungently to the sick. She fed them too,
roughly but well, and took the blood away—
and washed the dead, if there was that to do.
She told us children how the cows could sense
when their own calves were marked for butchering,
and how they lowed, their wordless eloquence
impossible to still with anything—
sweet clover, or her unremitting care.
She told it simply, but she faltered there.

Rosario on Sunday Morning

Oh no, not dreaming: clear as I hear you
now on our way to Mass, and the bells tolling,
I heard him calling in the dark last night.
Charo, he called me: I sat up in bed,
the smell of *madreselvas* everywhere,
heavy as the bunches he would bring
when he came courting, all those years ago.

Not dreaming, no: I never dreamed of him—
and seldom thought of him—in all those years
since I sent him away once and for all.
As for my sending him away, I said
all that I had to say then, as you know.
More is nobody's business, though there are
some in this town who may think otherwise.

He, and those honeysuckle bunches damp
from his mother's garden, week on week,
showed up on our front porch, where Mama stayed—
or Sara, or Susana—just to show
that the Alvarado girls, even the ripest,
would not be left alone with any suitor.

You knew my father, how he never said
outright what he could hint at while he chewed
on a cigar. And yet he told me once,
"When there's no bread, cassava's good enough."

Yes, from the start I knew they hoped I'd take him,
worn down by his scrubbed look. He was polite,
spoke as if he'd been schooled better than most,
but after crops and prices and the weather,
not much was left to say.

                              And in her way,
his mother courted me with smiles and small talk,
urged me to *recompense a good man's love:*
Amor con amor se paga, people say.
But love you take unwanted is no gift.
And if it were, why would one need to pay?

That's all of it, whatever some may think:
no quarrel, no advances to rebuff,
no secrets to uncover, his or mine.
I simply said, one day, it was no use
his waiting, waiting for what wouldn't fall,
when fresher fruit was out there for the picking,
at harvest dances and even private pews.

Before the rains, he left. And here I stayed—
odd how things happen—married, after all,
reared my two daughters and one bastard son
my late husband brought home, and then another,
taught the town's children over forty years,
with few regrets. Fewer, I'd say, than most,
and with less to do penance for than many
who'll kneel at the rail this morning for the host.

He could have stayed; but no, he was the one
who left—my porch, the town, his mother's house,
the farm, the island, all. If I believed
in country superstitions—but I don't—
I'd say he left the world itself last night.

Why did he come, unhindered by the lock,
in darkness, uninvited, and then call me—
Charo—by the one name nobody calls me?
Why did he say it with a voice that rose
out of a well of sorrow?

               And today,
although I've opened every window wide
to daylight breezes from the orange grove,
the honeysuckle smell lies like a pall
over my bed, as if a wall of sorrow
shut out the town and everything that's in it
but bells, as they might sound tolled under water.

Tú y yo

Ladan and Laleh Bijani . . . died . . . yesterday after
being surgically separated.
—New York Times, *July 9, 2003*

They're "Crown of Thorns" in English, image bent
on conjuring both pain and ornament;
but in my native soil and sunnier speech,
these silent coral bells grow, each from each
in amorous absorption, as *"tú y yo,"*
or "Thou and I." They do, as lovers know,
that sternest trick of all (at least they try):
remaining side by side until they die.

Those sisters who, joined at the head from birth,
flowered as one, could only guess the worth
of solitude denied them all their lives,
but knew deep in their bones (better than wives
and husbands do whose pairings may not last)
the joy of one shared future and one past.

What price such joys, such freedoms, as oppose
each other, when the route those sisters chose—
the scalpel—closes the journey? Journeys do,
of course, close, always: and the two-by-two
small floral marriages I trim and tend
collapse as single blossoms in the end.
I pick away the withered ones, and leave
the widowed on their stems. They do not grieve.

Luckily metaphors collapse as well,
and even doting gardeners can tell
these blooms that grace the thorns until they fall
have nothing much to say to us at all
about what loves we know—holy, profane,
rejoiced in for a time, outlived in pain.

Long Distance

What did we talk about when last we spoke?
Family gossip? Noses out of joint,
weddings and rumors? If we shared a joke,
I don't recall the punchline or the point,
only the silky texture of your speech,
your crafty pauses, the sly pitch and tone
of Spanish bantering, and how we each
warmed to the other's voice. If we had known
there would be no more casual talk so soon
after that call, would we have tried to frame
the words in earnest, though it was the tune
we sang to? And this evening, when word came,
I thought of both—how much was left to tell,
the mercy of not knowing. Just as well.

On a Gift of Dominican Mangoes
Confiscated at the Miami Airport

When the gruff agent
flipped them out of their gold foil
into the trash bag,

my heart fell with their
rosy amber lopsided
hearts sheathed in satin,

down where they sank with
confiscated scissors, knives
that would never slip

in to separate
their delicate ventricles,
dislodge the tender

moistness of their flesh,
release the tart turpentine
aroma that clings

to tongue and palate,
unsheathe their fibrous secret
core, their inner blond

syrupy parings.
Sweet others, long forgotten:
but oh, never these.

Choices

We gave my father what he wanted:
a grave in soil his love had haunted
because it held his elders' bones.
He sleeps at peace beneath worn stones.

My mother straddled a thin line.
That side was his, and this side mine:
the dead to whom his heart was true,
the young whose names she barely knew.

Here in my house, whose sunny rooms
are nothing like ancestral tombs,
I gave my mother what she chose:
Her ashes in their urn repose

where they are seldom left alone.
Three generations past her own
assault her sleep with games and toys.
I like to think she hears the noise.

"Home is the place where . . ."

No, more than "where they have to take you in,"
and no, not undeserved, not where you go
because there's nowhere else. Where you begin,
of course, but also where you end. And no,
not where your dead are buried, any more
than where they are who are not anywhere
yet, but whose names and faces you explore—
invent—inscribe in manuscripts of air.
The land that, like my mother, fed me first
and taught me the "true names" of everything;
this other, at whose breast I never nursed
but learned, instead, a second way to sing;
both, both are home—and where those call me from
who are already mine, though still to come.

Archaeology

This time, inside the wall:
a steady, high-pitched call,
but then slowing, and weaker.
Then, scattered loud dissent,
as if some tired speaker,
sick of an argument,
had nothing more to say
but said it anyway.

Silence the second day.
We called a man to check
the gutters and the flue,
the laths around the deck
(skunks have been known to dig
under and squirm through),
but no, this time, no sign
of anything so big.

Something looking to hide,
finding a hole so small
it can't be seen at all,
probably got inside
the attic, then went on
between the beams, to where
the studs descend, and there
contrived a nest, and died.

Past cure, they say, *past care*.
One day, when we're long gone,
if those who own the house
tear down our family room,
they well may find the mouse—
or bird, or other thing—
that found itself a tomb
house-hunting in the spring.

Are You Sure That You Want to Exist?

This jolt of metaphysics leaps at me
from the computer screen, in anapests
too jaunty for such probing inquiry,
unsettling for the scorn that it suggests,
its hint of threat. An instant's thought, of course,
corrects the reading: "exit," not "exist,"
not an offer to whisk me off by force,
but machine courtesy. Yet they persist,
the questions raised by what I chose to read:
Is anybody sure? Who has a say?
What other options are there, if indeed
I harbor doubts? I sometimes think I may,
but to so plain a query I repeat,
No exit, either! No! Do not delete!

Agenda

The house is still, but for the patient drum
of raindrops on the roof, as if some guest
who has forgotten where and when to come
were still looked for, though late. Under arrest

after a night's adventure, one dazed flapper
folds and unfolds her fading silks, between
the pane (you tilt it open to untrap her,
but she's too giddy) and the kitchen screen.

You turn the philodendron in its pot
and face the heart-shaped faces that it turns
as if to question you. But no, it's not
aware of you—of anything—and burns

only for water, which you bend to pour
under the tangled stems. The day, so spent
on such fool's errands as you're fashioned for,
leaves you by nightfall wondering where it went,

how else it could have gone, or to what ends—
assuming ends exist—that time that flew
cheerfully, casually, on work, on friends,
on what you thought it was there was to do.

Connection

How you begin is less important now
than in those days when, speaking to impress
some glib young stranger at a party, you
strained for a connection. You allow
silences now, and contradictions, less
careful to sound right, or tell it true,
or anything but listen. Which you do:
and finally the voice you hear is, yes,
familiar, and the conversation plays
as sequels to itself, so that you guess
more than the words will bear, learn to endow
with unsuspected weight the feathery phrase,
like an old couple's pillow talk. These days,
if it wants saying, it begins somehow.

Ousting the Murphys

Broken glass in a drawer, blade on a shelf,
nail upright in a crack between floor boards.
And in a dark basement corner, a trickle
of melting snow secret behind the wall

weeps day and night into the Murphys' carpet
and up into our alien bundles, seeps
into my wedding gown, photos of children
the house doesn't remember, grandparents
in the wrong garments posed in foreign light.

We clean, we dry, we order; but this house
mourns the Murphys, their faces vanished
forever from hall mirrors with their songs
and quarrels, their golf clubs and pillowed whispers.

We could demand obedience, nail our names
to blank walls like a manifesto, but
that would leave us besieged and stared at by
bought windows, ambushed by our strangeness.

Winning the house will cost humility,
the patience of moss. We'll have to feed it
our days gently, warm unfamiliar dishes,
stroke it with our sleep until it trusts us.

One morning these rooms must find us less dreadful
than absence, after all, better than silence;
knobs must learn to feel right, turn without fuss
and let us in at last, and we'll be home.

Discovery

Lifting the phone to call, he heard her laugh
on an extension: something had been said,
but what? and who had said it? He was half
tempted not to replace it in its bed
but hold it there by his astounded ear
to hear her laugh again in that old way
he had not heard since—when?—some distant year.
But also half afraid what she might say
into some other ear elsewhere. He dropped
the phone into its cradle, and the room
went loudly still, as if his life had stopped
like a stopped clock, as if it were a tomb
haunted by sounds he knew he used to know
but had forgotten missing long ago.

Look Long Enough

Look long enough at anything you know
and you will cease to know it. Or, not cease,
but struggle to reclaim it, wonder whether
you ever wore that shirt hanging just so
over your absent body, every crease
complex with shadows; or you pull a feather
from your old comforter, and altogether
altered by the flight of phantom geese,
familiar sheets repel you. Or two eyes
you've loved for years close in a daunting peace,
asleep, so that you listen for the flow
of breath, for words to help you recognize
a face you fail to find in this disguise,
although you knew it well, one look ago.

Retrospective

After so long, she still remembers how,
once, when he was courting her, he said,
"Watch out for me; I can be trouble." Now
it bewilders her how she misread
his words as an endearing lover's ploy,
a false confession meant to be denied
at once as such, laughed at, and—oh, the joy
of it!—silenced with kisses. On the ride
home, now, from a rare day with friends—not his
but hers, and he resents the visit—they
are silent. Love's not blind: it sees what is,
she thinks, but turns from it, waves it away,
plays dumb on purpose. And she laughs again.
How well she gets the joke she missed back then.

Grandson, Reading

Ambrose, now mastering the book,
no longer needs
to memorize how letters look,
or use his index finger as a hook
to string them like loose beads:
in short, he reads.

Now pictures seem, at best, a frill,
an outgrown toy.
It is the printed words that thrill,
voices that travel with him where he will,
a solitary joy.
A lucky boy,

for whom so many authors wait,
all still unread!
And some of them, obscure or great,
will seem to guess his thoughts and glimpse his fate,
as if they, in his head,
read him instead.

For now, though, this is all: two covers
part to engage
this reader's soul—like any lover's,
lost in the landscape over which it hovers,
no matter what his age—
page after page,

right index at the ready, tip
poised not to miss
an instant on the turn, but slip
at once to the next page, his careful lip
shaping, much like a kiss,
each word, like this.

Little Red Hen

Yes, Hen, you're right: give no free pass
to members of the leisure class
who angle for your unpaid labor.
And yet, consider: there's the neighbor
who's elderly or unemployed,
or in bad health, or has enjoyed
few opportunities. Does merit
precisely weighed enlist the spirit,
or is it need, or social duty?
Is there not something much like beauty
in serving, with no compensation
but saintly joy—that odd elation—
precisely those who, least deserving,
will find the unearned good unnerving
until they've passed it on in kind?
So Heaven may work upon the mind
of man—and maybe dog and cat.
But, Hen, your guarded, tit-for-tat,
ethical but unsaintly rule
is learned in a much older school,
Where even bread from wheat you planted
is not at all taken for granted.

The Wolf

Across two pages of my grandson's book
he leaps, bristling with speed, toothed like a saw,
intent on Piggy, his mad yellow look
igniting cloudy fireworks of straw.
Ambrose is two years old, and can surmise
how this must end: clearly he does not need
the words he has not heard. He shuts his eyes—
now brimming—and the book, and pleads, "No read,"
and burrows in the safety of my lap,
where Piggy, too, would have been safe. No doubt
Ambrose believes as much; he takes his nap
without more thought of the fierce, hungry snout
possibly trapped in texts he need not know,
or boiling in the pot where bad things go.

Dying Huge Dragon

*Colored marker on plastic laminate, 34 in x 22 in,
Newburyport, private collection of the artist's
grandmother.*

This thick brown line
is all the hide he owns.
It's not enough—
despite tall wings and spiky orange stuff
bristling along his spine—
to shield him from the stones
(or are they spears?) that fly
to make him die.

Look at his length
and breadth, from snout to tail;
look at the thin
stick men half-hidden by the grass they're in.
They pitch, with all their strength,
black scribbles that impale
the monster's parts, and spread
splotches of red.

Brave, though in pain,
his eyes now blear and dim,
in self-defense
he spits a cloud of scarlet flames, immense,
but useless in that rain
of spots that spatter him
and smash into the kegs
that are his legs.

The artist now
steps back, pauses to see
the work he's done,
the colors of the bloody scene that run
on hands and cheeks and brow,
as if he aimed to *be*
—and not simply *portray*—
hunt, hunter, prey.

"Things That Go"

Hoop and arrow,
wheel and dart,
kite and rocket,
stream and heart;

fan and motor,
mill and train,
waterwheel,
remembered pain;

summer, autumn,
winter, spring;
desire and
desired thing;

suns that burn
and rains that weep;
children you once
rocked to sleep.

Fourteen

She moves as if her body were a shoot
uncertain of its upward-destined route,
so newly-sprung from Earth as to be still
evasive of the sky, slow to fulfill
the rising impetus that sun inspires.

She moves as if a rumor of green fires,
rising through her stem, spread to the lace
of silky sleeves, and then her petaled face
were lifted in the tumult of the air,
abashed to hear hosannahs everywhere.

For Lincoln Gideon

Beautiful boy named after men so great
(both born to wield the law, to liberate,
to lead great people through harsh times), I wonder
how such smooth, silky cheeks square with such thunder!
But never mind: your life is yours to make,
yours the selection of what risks to take,
what wars to wage, with weapons of your choice:
the pen, the scalpel, or the singer's voice,
the dancer's leap, the leap the physicist
makes in his mind—it's such an endless list!
And, Lincoln Gideon, whatever path
you choose to follow, may the aftermath
of your long faring—childhood to old age—
be one bright chronicle of decent page
after page, as sweet as it is long,
to prove your parents did not name you wrong,
but to confirm you, with a double trust,
daring, like Gideon, and like Lincoln, just.

State of the Art

The box in which some large device arrived
a week or two ago has been transformed
into a starship. In it, two small boys
manage to fit, just barely. It deploys
instruments so refined that they've survived
meteors and asteroids on scary trips
beyond our galaxy, thanks to twelve tips
of tin-foiled ice-cream sticks secured with tape.

On all four cardboard flaps on top, trim panels
laid out in crisp black marker indicate
velocity, location, time and date,
and monitor connections with Earth channels.

Exploding novas and black holes have stormed
this craft. But so sagely designed
is it, so ably captained by its two
commanders, so well served by its brave crew
(three bears, a tortoise, a red-spotted frog,
and Grandma, who provides crackers and cheese)
that every hazard ends with an escape.

Ambrose enters all those in the ship's log,
with Perry's illustrations: art combined
(da Vinci's records look a lot like these)
with science, to instruct the centuries.

Shelter

How clever of my neighbor to devise
this little cage of nets in his front yard
to keep his children—and the toys they guard—
safe in the larger cage of Papa's eyes.

He's strung it between trees, by curtain hooks
from which four airy walls hang down: inside,
a wooden pony small enough to ride,
if you are small enough to read cloth books.

Light rain has grizzled the straw mane, and lends
weight to the text of flowery ABC's;
today rider and reader, on their knees,
are coloring indoors with noisy friends.

All of this bounded by the flimsiest fence.
Its maker knows the stranger passing through,
armed with a knife, would know just what to do
to make a mockery of confidence.

And still my clever neighbor girds about
his irreplaceable—his priceless—things,
as if he knew some charm in sticks and strings
to keep the treasure in, the danger out.

A Neighbor Speaks His Mind

for Fran Schreiber

There is a lady lives beside the garden
where I have built a nest and reared my chicks
who keeps the garden green: she is its warden,
clearing, in spring, dry brush and wintry sticks,

in summer, feeding. And she feeds us too,
so well that both my timid mate and I,
at her approach, approach her—knowing who
and what our neighbor is—and do not fly.

Her eyes are gray, I think, and gray her hair,
as soft as down, and all her motions kind,
as, bent on loving errands here and there,
her every gesture speaks a gentle mind.

There is a man with her who seems her friend—
and more than friend, perhaps—who guards the place,
and they exchange light noises without end
and trade warm looks, lip-touching face to face.

My mate is my delight, but I confess,
watching this lady closely, as I can,
she conjures Leda to my mind, and yes,
I half regret I cannot be that man.

Believer

for Tim Murphy

My friend insists he wants me to be saved.
He argues that my soul will come to grief
unless it's rescued from my unbelief
by Jesus—though I'm fairly well behaved,

and not, as sinners go, a perfect ten.
My friend's a poet—hunter, too—at both
pursuits relentless in the chase, and loath
to forfeit any prey: the souls of men,

phrases that say what he would have them sing,
four ducks downed with one shell (for he shoots true!)—
all must be saved, by Feeney from the slough,
or from Hell's brink by prayer. He wants each thing

retrieved, and labors daily to that end,
with gun or syntax or with beads to tell,
till, like a poem, all is finished well
and safely bagged to please his holy Friend.

I've never touched a soul or aimed a gun,
and as for gods, although I know by name
several dozen, I've enjoyed the same
benign neglect, so far, from every one.

If I need saving—and it well may be,
though I don't know from what or by what means—
let it be here among familiar scenes,
by friends who choose to kneel and pray for me.

Oh, Wow!

Candid View

Clearly, this is no Helen: not one skiff
would have been launched by the pinched smile, the stiff
hand shading one eye from summer sun,
and one eye tearing; it is 'fifty-one,
I guess, when this was taken. And I knew—
my mother warned me—that it would not do
to count on beauty, or what looks procured.
Luckily love came early, and endured.

The warning, I learned later—many years
after the girl I was had dried those tears—
had been *pro forma*, issued to prevent
the sin of vanity. The same intent
had led my mother's mother to the lies
that kept her, also, dim in her own eyes,
told not from malice, but in virtue's name.

The series closed with me: no daughters came
to be kept modest at a price so steep.
Lucky, since what we're taught is what we keep,
if we're taught early. I have handsome boys;
telling them so is one among my joys.

Another is discovering—though late—
how not to credit words that devastate,
if they are spoken by misguided love
that once endured what it is guilty of.
And yes, one more: the pleasure, long deferred,
of finding my young face, of which I heard
such painful things, deserving of no less
than any face we would not curse or bless.
I wonder—having cursed it long ago—
what else would have been comforting to know.

Hammock

Parenthesis in whose first arc you lie
face up, as if some sentence, earth to sky,
chose you for subject . . . then, with odd reserve,
left out all predicate from curve to curve.
How kind this author is, how diplomatic,
to leave you barely named and enigmatic,
a pure ellipsis, like a day at dawning!
Outside, midafternoon, a leafy awning,
midsummer's lush monotony of green;
cicadas chirr, voluble but unseen.
With what beguiling ease the hammock's side-
to-side and broomlike motion, like the wide
cursive of children, sweeps away the shade
out of whose deepening the night is made.
What simple joy to wait for sleep in this
suspended, snug, one-half parenthesis!

Choosing a Seat

Face backwards and you'll see where you've just been.
Closing like scissor blades, that point pursues
the train until a turn lopsides it in
and out of sight. Curves are the only news.

That would be restful, but for an uneasy
tug on the body, suctioning it out
of the seat's hard security, the queasy
pull of speed in reverse, a kind of doubt.

Grinding into the station settles that,
though, and the backbone hugs its place again.
If you face forward you move sure and flat
past rushing lights, dark columns, working men

strobed by trick vision like prophetic dreams,
hypnotic once they're gone. But as you near
a stop, deceleration pries you, seems
to invite you out, whispers *You're here.*

Sit sideways and you hardly move at all,
intent on neighbors' newspapers, asleep,
or contemplating nothing. You recall
what someone said, wonder if you should keep

this or that promise, count letters in some ad.
You rock sideways a little, like a child
on some narcotic shoulder. That's not bad,
if what you like is passing time, beguiled

by trifles, who knows what. In any case,
whatever your choice of posture, chances are
you'll stand, wishing yourself some other place,
and travel just as fast and just as far.

Halfway

Halfway between from and to,
where strangers and familiars meet,
a woman that I not-quite-knew
boarded the train and took a seat.

We faced each other, knee to knee;
the landscape, as it flickered by,
was first a blur a house a tree
and then a hook from eye to eye.

And each, admonished by that look,
which only for an instant deigned
to find the other wanting, took
refuge in the calm she feigned.

Where would each be at journey's end,
wearing her days like chains or wings,
those nights the other would not spend,
like heavy costly careless rings?

The woman I am not—but might,
if not for chance, once have become—
stepped out into the failing light,
halfway between to and from.

Celebration

A toast to our five oldest friends:
those that surround,
delight and wound and make amends.
Begin with sound,

music that is what language only means,
how voice embraces.
Then sight—the blues and browns and greens
that every place is,

motion, and the come and go of light,
dust dancing in it.
And then the whiff in flight
the very minute

we breathe it in from soil, resinous wood—
or steaming bowl
in which the tongue discovers *good*.
Think how the soul—

proudly nothing—nevertheless
becomes aware
of all we need to dress
its naked air.

And then that intimate adviser: skin,
which all our days
instructs the body's *out* and *in*;
think how the mind surveys,

under such guidance, everything it knows.
A toast, a toast to the one life it spends
blessed by the tutelage of those
five mortal friends.

Observation

Focus on them head on, and things appear
strange in the masks they wear, which is the mask
they are. Perceived in space too bright, too clear,

a spoon, a glove, a clock at its dull task,
seem ominously edged, as if they knew
secrets they might tell, if you could ask;

or might confide—could you persuade them to—
the text they gloss, miracles you might work
through them, if they but told you what to do.

Now lower the shades to tinge the air with dark,
or focus askew, turn to the left or right
a little, and they will lose their stark

premonitory stare. In that forgiving light
of imprecision, familiar objects wear
the common look granted by common sight.

Neither half-lit nor in the purest air
will they reveal what is not there, yet there.

אנר

My name, in Hebrew, with a cast of three,
all facing left: one waves and moves on, striding;
the second—upright, as if gravity
nailed down that big flat foot to old abiding
ground—may move, but slowly; and the last,
leaning to look ahead, is neither still
nor moving, but alert, as if to cast
cold vision forward before chance or will
can lure on or compel. Their names are Resh,
Nun, Aleph—R, N, A—which, although terse
because one vowel's missing, somehow mesh
to the way Hebrew spells me, in reverse.
The friend (poet and artist, both) who sent
me this can read the script, and knows the sound
conveys no plot and harbors no intent,
but I enjoy the joke her eye has found,
which tells a truth by accident, sheds light
that one-eyed reason calls the poet's sin.
Of course, I read it wrong, from left to right:
how does it say I end, and how begin?

On the Curious, Intimate and Reactive Nature of Human Identity

A man who hates me takes me for a Jew—
or he pretends to, since it gives him leave
to satisfy a private grudge, and pair
it with scorn he is committed to.
The yellow star he wants me forced to wear
I would accept with pride. He hopes to grieve
me, spitting out my husband's Jewish name.
I was not born to what he thinks that "shame,"
but claim the right to share it, as my due:
the hate that aimed it makes me wish it true.

Seasoning

Moving from right to left like Hebrew prayers,
I season supper: garlic, pepper, salt,
oregano, perhaps, whose tang of farmyard
beckons me away to fields long built on,
to pots and spoons long rusted by slow rains
under another sky, to tables set
for those who will not share with me again
the daily psalm and sacrament of food.

From right to left I season, left to right
I put the condiments away. Such sleights of mind
are how I signal memory home again
to this dish, to keep from seasoning twice.

Where does it hide, this dissolution, wanderlust
that springs to find us after the first goodbyes
and the last weddings? There's not a perfume, not
a ribbon of music that doesn't wind somewhere
away from this hour and place, as if all roads
conspired to lead us out of what Rome we have,
what room we know.

                    Well, I'm prepared: from right
to left, like *kaddish,* I sprinkle salt on
this flesh, all flesh; then, ecumenical,
I cross it left to right in token of
hope's gospel, to hail the second coming—
or the sun, whichever remembers to come first.

Oh, Wow!

What joy it mimes in tireless repetition,
the heart, mugging its echocardiogram:
Oh, Wow! from secret mouths. Now the technician
refocuses, and shifts the scene I am,
shows me which is the mitral valve, whose touch,
not quite across the current, lets the flow
feather back on itself, but not too much.
Take a deep breath and hold it; let it go.
How jubilant, this cheering no one hears,
astonishing bewilderment the heart
rehearses day to day and all its years—
gossip relayed to every waiting part—
and over such stale news, from birth to now,
as drawing breath: *Oh, Wow! Oh, Wow! Oh, Wow!*

Shower Talk

To you who feed on what I scrub away
I say, *Bon appétit!* As you all may,

to lesser feeders who ingest your parts
to nourish their own livers, lungs and hearts,

assuming such in customers so small
they wear that last disguise: nothing at all.

Nothing doesn't exist, of course: what's there
is always Something, hiding everywhere,

stalking its prey, or waiting in the drain
for what may bless it if it prays for rain.

Something posing as Nothing draws me out
of my warm water, almost makes me shout

into the void eternally receding,
"You there, busy at once serving and feeding,

what feeds the need that drives the servers too?
What eats whatever eats what feeds on you?"

Retrievals

Well, I've had two. (And I've been told they come
in threes: three sons, in countless tales, who save
the kingdom on the third try, after some
bumbling; three wishes; and of course the grave,

cheated on day three! Who, after such
clear evidence, can doubt it?) Just last night,
that stranger at the theater bent to touch
my shoulder, as I heard his whispered, light,

"Madam, you dropped this," and felt, back in my hand,
my little watch, still ticking—oh, what luck!—
no worse off for the failure of its band.
And there's still more: later, at home, I tuck

my hand into the pocket of a coat
I seldom wear, and here's the wallet missed
and hunted for in vain, a folded note—
urgent, too late—and an old grocery list.

The signs are sure: I'm listening for him,
that third messenger, pimply, gangly, wearing
his cashier's apron over the seraphim
plumage of his holy trade, but bearing

treasure back to me: "Madam, your youth!
Your memory, your sight! Your life's designs!
Some incandescent words that tell the truth
as never told before, in fourteen lines!

I found them on the counter where you paid
for eggs, a head of lettuce, and six rolls."
Or maybe, "Are these yours, promises made
and still to be fulfilled? And these old souls

safe in their shrouds, tagged in our Lost and Found,
still murmuring your name in the close air?"
Why not look for retrievals, search the ground,
the past—pockets to ransack everywhere!

Familiar Faces

Familiar faces you can seldom name,
in thought, as in some supermarket aisle,
rush toward you, then goodbye—always the same.

At first, alarm; and then a flush of shame
because you're not sure who's behind that smile:
so many faces now that you can't name!

They nod, as if establishing a claim
to be remembered here and now. Meanwhile,
you wonder if they're wondering the same,

doing the alphabet—that silly game
in which you flip through memory's tattered file
hoping some letter will retrieve a name.

Sometimes it works. Sometimes the social frame
almost succeeds: *That was the Juvenile*
Books author you once read with on the same

panel, or . . . *the junior-high "old flame"*
who exercised his most transparent guile
to kiss you. But how could you lose his name!

Sometimes you sense what distances they came
to visit you in dreams, wearing the style
of other decades, calling you by name.
It's you, you think—*but who? and still the same*!

Confession

My hair is thinning. More, each day,
cleaves to the brush, forsakes the head,
its lush, dark handfuls now, instead,
meager and gray.

A very minor grief, it's true,
when plague and famine, death and war
bereave so many of much more.
Yet, grieve I do.

Holding the mirror to my crown,
observing how the landscape's changing
compels some artful rearranging—
it gets me down,

though I'm ashamed to be caught weeping
over such paltry stuff as curls—
as if the crowns we wear as girls
were meant for keeping.

How Sullen She's Become

How sullen she's become lately, the body,
how vengeful over trifles: one step missed
climbing an unlit stair will earn you bloody
bruises, swollen throbbing at the wrist
you fell on. Once she ran to do your bidding
like a young bride; now, like an aging spouse,
the body sulks, jealous and still brooding
over those decades spent keeping your house,
your schedule, your accounts, while you philandered
after the soul. The body's bent on going,
one of these days, to teach you what you've wondered:
what's left without her lifelong service, knowing
how well she served you once, without the love
you give that soul you're so enamored of.

Red Shoes

I bought red shoes the other day.
They were on sale, which can't excuse
purchasing something so *outré*.
I bought red shoes,

knowing they're likely to confuse
people who've known me day to day
for the strict ways and quiet views

of those who seldom go astray
or turn up in the precinct news.
But then again, who knows? I may.
I bought red shoes.

Losers Weepers

I've lost another umbrella, gone the way
of gloves and earrings, books, keys, my blue scarf.
I'd ask at the Lost and Found, but the people there
resent it, as if loss were a kind of tax
due to one's use of time and space: bad form,
bad citizenship, asking for refunds.

Things seldom turn up, anyway; sometimes
they do, but never quite as you lost them,
still usable or even halfway fit.
I tell myself, "It was on its last legs
and not something I prized much." But the truth is,
any loss cuts into us a little.

Is it because, like Navajos, we're afraid
to leave bits of ourselves among strangers
who may suck in our spirits through them? No,
it's not fear of the stranger who'll stay dry
under my umbrella, nor of the rain
I'll get caught in without it, that troubles me.

It's the crumbling, maybe, the termite dust
trailing me from movie to coffee shop,
whispering everywhere that gravity's gone slack,
that pieces are coming loose like shingles.
Time to strike a balance, add up the tally:
I've done my share of finding, as well as losing.

It was I who found the chiseled Mycenaean dagger
that summer at Stonehenge, just barely there
on the weathered rock, where some Greek workman,
thinking of home, signed history with his loss.
I understand him, having lost a whole town
once, inhabitants, narrow streets and all,

like a wallet left behind in a phone booth.
And I found a skink in the woods once, scooped
out of his mossy room into my hand
where he lay black and orange, like Halloween
candy, both trick and treat. I put him back
under his stone roof, but memory kept him,

his licorice eyes and his damp house to boot.
Not bad, in a world where even the luckiest finders
are seldom keepers. Well, taxes are fair—
or so I tell myself, willing to learn
that in this galaxy, at least, you get
what you pay for like a good citizen.

November

Those yellow flags the birches fly—
those not surrendered yet—still cling
as if in hope, against a sky
so clear it augurs early spring;

the day that was an empty cup
brims over with the ghost of green,
as if the act of looking up
itself created what is seen.

And, though surprised, the senses, too,
believe—briefly, almost—until
reason points out how very few
those leaves are, how the birds are still,

and how the oaks are bare and brown.
But having rearranged the year,
why knuckle under, settle down
to any narrow now and here?

Why not, instead, accept it all:
hope, and the truth it differs from,
midwinter spring and May in fall,
the gone for good, the still to come.

Trifocals

A friend complains his eyes are failing. Yes,
I can believe it. At this age, I too
lean toward the lamp and tilt the shade, and guess
at punctuation on the page. Now blue—
like black and green—is one more shade of brown,
and must be scrutinized before I choose
garments to put on, or else a clown
wearing my face goes forth, dressed to amuse.
Disgraceful, but I'm starting not to care—
or to care less—when, startled from a nap,
I find the window darkening up there
above some headline shouting from my lap,
and almost think I like the column better
for the pale ghosts that play around each letter.

To My Good Left Hand

Like a shy child not counted on for much
beyond the simplest problems to get right,
you're hesitant and slow, your awkward touch
uncertain when it gauges heavy, light,
too far, too near. Your comb's a clumsy rake;
the pen you coax to write forgets its place;
the spoon you stir with raises waves that make
you strain after a kind of makeshift grace.
Apprentice, understudy, you who stand
for all who are least likely to make good,
what will you do now that the other hand—
your clever twin—is swaddled stiff as wood,
with twice the weight of failure left for you?
It's hard, I know, I know; I've been there too.

To My Gall Bladder

Is this goodbye to you, who for so long
have shared my days and nights, so near my heart
I thought that we were one? But I was wrong.
What guilt—and whose—is tearing us apart?
Is it my long affair with cheese that grates
on you? My glass of wine—or maybe two—
with dinner? My refusal to lift weights
or do the treadmill thing? And yes, it's true
I've had you tracked with cameras, to see
what you've been up to; but too late, no use:
too much has soured between you and me
that I can't stomach. I must cut you loose.
Had we confided sooner . . . who can tell?
No more hard feelings, though: I wish you well.

Too

December thirty-one: too rich a spread,
too much of what there is, too strange, too bright,
too many dishes tasted that instead
of filling, feed the hunger, every bite
promising to be perfect—but not quite;
too much to want, when nothing but excess
will do, spiraling skyward like a kite.
And too late now to wish it any less.

Too many pearls on gold and silver thread
for needlework begun by young delight,
finished by duty, if not left for dead:
this tapestry, that kinship starved on spite,
those pages never written, safe and white
with cowardice, unwilling to confess
what the light does that makes the dark contrite.
And too late now to wish it any less.

Too many books meant to be read, unread
on shelves youth stocked when it believed it might;
too much meant to be said but left unsaid
that wanted saying when the time was right;
too much said wrong, too much held close and tight
that should have been let go, have been largesse
flung free at once and never kept from flight.
And too late now to wish it any less.

Face in the mirror, reading by cold light
the lines that spell your history, come bless
what one more year decrees this final night.
Much too late now to wish it any less.

The Closing Year

Beside the Merrimack, in white,
cocooned from winds they hope to ride,
the huddled boats are sleeping tight,
marooned on stilts above the tide.

Above the streets—Federal, State,
Pleasant, and High—four steeples stand,
on guard over the city's fate,
in which they mean to have a hand.

Now autumn's copper days are gone;
the maples and the oaks are bare.
Their branches shiver and put on
the thinnest coat of birdless air.

Squirrel and mouse, each tends his town:
so much to scamper for, to hoard,
to drag high up or wrestle down
for warmth in winter, bed and board.

And on their lawns, now brown and sere,
neighbors look up at clouds that pass,
and then retreat indoors to peer
and mime hellos through double glass.

The river, though, goes where it will.
In every season, swift or slow,
it skirts the shade of silent mills,
mirrors old bridges from below,

lapping, at last, the city's docks
where seagulls cry above the bay,
and ripples back from harbor rocks,
as if to go, as if to stay.

Time Travel

There's no way back the way we came.
Were we too simple, when we thought
the route was simple? Soon the same

roads, in hindsight, wore a frame
darkened, as by some lens that caught
what we forgot. But on we came,

beguiled with nightfall's harmless game
at first, the shadows playful, not
threatening. They seemed the same,

those roads we knew, whose only aim,
we thought, was leading where they ought.
Looking back now, the way we came

led us astray. Are we to blame
for signposts that we failed to spot
as daylight failed? Is this the same

failure that alters what we name,
misses the trail and twists the plot?
There's no way back: the ways we came—
or is it we?—are not the same.

Bridges

Bridge on the soundboard of that old guitar
whose silent strings you never learned to play;
bridge between melodies, motifs that say
there is a leap to make from near to far;
bridge on the deck from which the sailor's star
shunned you by night and puzzled you by day;
bridge for the billiard cue to find its way—
if daring sends it where the options are.

Game for a cryptic foursome; path that goes
dust-dry above the river's roiling mass;
brief bony hyphen linking, on the nose,
two eyes between which visions never pass;
slim yoke from lens to lens; safe in repose
beside old sleepers, dentures in a glass.

In Darkened Rooms

To apprehend an object in the dark,
focus on where it's not: a little right
or left of anywhere. Without a spark
to see by, it will sidle into sight,
as if the eye had wrought a counterfeit.

A man who thought he loved me told me that.
I knew he didn't—and was glad of it—
and told him so, by way of caveat:
knowing how hope creates what it consumes,
I wanted no false hopes feeding on me.

His face escapes me now, but memory
surprises me sometimes in darkened rooms.

Flipping Through

She will not see you here,
admiring the severe
black gown in which she poses
beside a bowl of roses.

The roses, she, the man
whose deep-set eyes you scan
for some familial look,
live only in this book,
where no one thought to spell
names known—and loved—so well
it seemed superfluous
to jot them down for us.

You turn the page at last
on all the nameless past,
inventing so-and-so
to make them yours. But no,
they're not—could not have been—
outside the frames they're in.

One day this will be you:
a woman staring through
film at which strangers stare.
You will not see them there.

The Bargain

Late Call

for Paul Korwin

As when a friend—before I lock the door,
rinse out the cups and pour the dregs away—
turns in the street to wave and make one more
parting suggestion (*Let's have dinner, say,
tomorrow or next week*) and then moves on,
your telephone recorder—in your voice!—
delights my ear by proving you're not gone,
and gives me one last instant to rejoice.
But no, you are not home, this is not you,
only the words a clever tape may keep,
but not your head thrown back to laugh, your blue
clear eyes. You want my name *after the beep*,
ask me to say it slowly, if I would,
promise to call me back. I wish you could.

Lighthouse, with Poet Brandishing His Hat

for Alfred Dorn

This is the poet posing, hat in hand,
not as a beggar may when thanks are due
to charitable strangers passing by,
but as a champion in the ring may stand
brandishing laurels; it's a jaunty cue
the crowd responds to, raising heaven-high
the tribute of its hoarse, frenetic cry.
Behind the poet, shouldering the blue
pavilions of the air, the lighthouse peers
over the bard, as if to say, *I, too,*
rally the fearful, like this firebrand,
to dare the monsters born of wordless fears.
For every passing craft I lift, like cheers,
my wreath of light above the darkened strand.

For Ronnie, One Wall Away

Imagining your daughters and their tears
as you are laid to rest this soft spring day,
I resurrect, out of our simple years,
the near-sisters we were, picture the way
one wall did not divide my house and yours
but join them, as a membrane in the heart
may seem to sever blood from blood, but pours
a single flow that quickens every part.
How I remember the sweet din they made—
your girls, my little boys—in the safe green
they littered with their toys, under the shade
crabapple and wild cherry cast between
our kitchen windows. Yes, and how I yearn
for faith that could believe such things return.

People Who Give You Things

People who give you things they meant to keep
but can't, because it's time to let them go—
what do you tell them? "I prefer my sleep
not stitched with your regrets"? Or, "Sorry, no,
my closet's full to bursting: there's no room inside
for faded wishes, for the tight despair
you've tried to squeeze around me like a hide,
and I with so much of my own to wear!"
But how can you refuse them, when they come
night after night with armfuls of the stuff
they made the wardrobe of your childhood from,
left over from their own—and still enough
to dress the present—and the future, too,
stuck with boxes to pick through after you.

For Robert, Without a Pass

How many years ago was it my joy
to sign you in on the term's opening day,
wearing both baby fat that clothed a boy
and a man's heart, and with so much to say
in terms you hoped would label you bizarre?
And so you were, and gifted, and unarmed,
except with humor. An unlikely star,
you doubled—knight and clown—wielding a charmed
vocabulary honed with wit. Your papers
rewarded all the patience they wore thin
with verbal pratfalls, and your very capers
planted ideas you toppled with a grin.
But what to make, now, of your cutting class,
taking this *incomplete*, without a pass!

For Ginger, Who Hummed

Last night I heard you humming at your stove,
slapping about in slippers on the slate
of your Southwestern kitchen. How it drove
sorrow away to smell it, watch you grate
your pungent magic on the layered green
of jalapeños! But the pearly light
of this New England morning fell between
your final hour and what I wished by night.
How comforting to think—if so I thought—
that on some morning out of time, some place
beyond departures, we might both be brought
back to the taste, the wooden spoon, your face
absorbed in work you loved, your slippered feet,
the joy of common days both brief and sweet.

Which of the Arts You Mastered

for David Berman

Which of the arts you mastered—through a life
rich in accomplishments—defines you best?
The lawyer's art, that talent you possessed
for finding order where disorder's rife,
in human judgment? Or your scholar's way
with words—those of Lucretius or Saint Paul,
or ours—you studied? You enriched them all.
Or your musician's gift for making play
out of the labor of confronting pain?
Wit, poet, verbal jeweler, and much more:
oenologist and gourmet chef whose door
opened with joy, who said, "Come soon agayne,"
like that, to friends who mourn you. As we should.
Come soon agayne indeed. We wish you could.

Casual Losses

Falling, the cage made cozy for the bird
flew open, spilling out his gaudy toys.
The child threw herself over it, but heard,
already growing thin, a chilling noise:
his chatter, playful, through the neighbor's tree,
spiraling into vacancies of blue.
Useless, that hour spent in agony
jingling forsaken bells he loved: she knew
he had adventured farther than both sight
and hearing, over all the fields of air,
having forgotten her and the delight
of millet in his cup, the homely care
she clung to, still attentive to discern
the whirr of his impossible return.

Afterthoughts

Not only what you said, but how,
wounded me then, and rankles now,
when I remember with what good
precise replies in mind I stood
without a word, to scotch the row.

A wasted chance, if what we say
is meant for use, to clear away—
like rake in spring or housewife's broom—
the trash that clutters yard or room.
But that's not how you spoke that day.

You spoke to pile the compost deep
under whose weight old rancors sleep,
and I—too fond of peace by half,
too civil—was content to laugh
and let my honest answers keep.

Such are the ill-played scenes that drive
imagination to contrive
alternate lines more nearly true.
And yet who knows what I would do
but what I did, were you alive.

Trinacria

On the Day of the Dead, all of us children would ask each other,
"Chi ti purtaru li morti (What did the dead bring you)?"
—Mariangela Sechi, Tour Guide, Sicily, October, 2001

I. Crypt of the Capuchin Monks

This site we were not shown: the catacombs
beneath Palermo. Maybe our young guide,
considering our ages, feared that tombs
would chill old bones, and chose the harborside.
"Impressionable people are advised
not to visit"—so this guidebook warns—
"these long rows of dead bodies." Solemnized
by their stiffness on slabs no art adorns,
here they are now, in black and white, a scene
more grisly as depicted than it may,
in fact, have seemed had we been led between
the dead and found them, lit by common day,
reduced to life dimensions by the eye.
It is the unseen thing we magnify.

II. Sicilian Puppet Theater

A painted box whose walls are hung with row
on row of wooden warriors. Or, at least,
their heads are wood, their armor tin, aglow
with daily burnishing; their robes, a feast
of silk and braid. Their faces, noble, fierce,
distinguish Paladin from Saracen,
all eager to be skewered, or to pierce
a dragon, or unseam a thousand men.
Above the stage, what each encounter means
is clarified in brave, if crude, cartoons.
The skilled *puparo* works behind the scenes:
when infidels attack, the maiden swoons
and heroes strut because he works the rods
that activate their zeal for rival gods.

III. Temple at Segesta

If gods exist, here's how they should appear:
not in descent through lightning or the sun,
or winged for conquest, but ascent. As here—
Segesta, where the building seems not done
by labor but by spirit—columns rise
like harvests into clear Sicilian blue,
unquarried and self-made. In this disguise,
the gods belong to us, as grasses do.
But nothing rises, here or anywhere,
this cleanly from the soil without some cost:
slaves left their names, inaudible as air,
invisible on stones they worked, embossed
like soldiers' graves dimpling some farmer's fields,
their blood on everything the landscape yields.

IV. Cathedral of Monreale

Newly created, Adam takes a nap.
The Lord, clad in mosaics, by the power
of His right hand, makes Eve (about to clap,
apparently, or maybe pick a flower
from the small tree before her) spring to life
out of the sleeper's side. Adam has missed
the moment—the emergence of his wife—
and turns away, as one who will insist
henceforth, as the firstborn, on special terms.
Elsewhere, each panel gleams with hopeful gold
from which the posture of each saint confirms
the glory of God's work. Here only, cold,
uneasy light illuminates the scene
tucked in this shady corner of the green.

V. Piazza Armerina, Villa Erculia

The Villa's mistress is immortal here,
standing between her children and two maids:
five bodies balanced to convey austere
but gracious presences, their faces shades
of small mosaics blended dark to light
so deftly they're alive. We're told her name:
Eutropia; Fausta, left; Maxentius, right;
unnamed, the maids, probably girls who came
from the far provinces, both east and west.
From Africa, selected with great care,
workmen who were reputed as the best
were brought to lay these tiles. They're shown elsewhere,
dressed like the countrymen they left behind.
Look how their work conceals, reveals, the mind.

VI. Villa Erculia: The Small Hunt

Look how this wounded huntsman, dripping gore—
libations to the dead!—as his alert
companion thrusts his spear into the boar,
turns from the dogs that snap, the drops that spurt.
The blood is crimson—nothing ghostly here—
and figures cast small shades; the sun is high;
the tusks are white, as is the man whose fear
has made him pale. But no, he will not die.
This time good friends have saved him; blood he's lost
will be replaced in time. Nearby he sees
that cooks are at their work, the goose is tossed
on coals to grill under those poplar trees,
the steward pours. Not yet among the dead!
How fine, this living, sharing wine and bread.

VII. Catania

Wendy, widowed and British, lifts her green
umbrella as a signal to move on
through gray Catania. Idle old men lean
on crumbling walls, gawking until we've gone
up the cathedral steps to view the tomb
that holds Bellini, dead at thirty-four.
We hear his story, and in deeper gloom
the legend of Saint Agatha, that poor
dismembered child whose ancient martyred flesh
has triumphed to this day over the grave.
Having seen the saint's hands, still sweet and fresh,
Wendy credits the spirit's power to save.
At the town market she inspects the fish,
buys shrimp and mussels for her midday dish.

VIII. For You, Mariangela

For you, Mariangela, this sheaf of pages,
not from the dead, but from the living who
trailed you past worn stones and down the ages
to learn what gifts the old bequeath the new.
That field where Hades ravished his young wife,
the seven boulders Polyphemus tossed
to crush Odysseus, rowing for his life,
those temples where old strangers crossed and crossed
each other's routes, raised crosses, and remained,
divided and inseparable as sand—
all that you showed us—and the ash that rained
down from Mount Etna on the ravaged land.
Your countrymen resettle each year's pyre.
They know each harvest is the gift of fire.

Nothing

for Yala

"Nothing," she says, "nothing is wrong. Come in."
The friend from out of town steps in around her,
watches her lock the door from the inside,
as always, and embraces her old friend.
"But what is this?" the guest says, pointing at
the bandage—makeshift, a handkerchief
folded and pinned to hide one eye. "Let's see."
Slow, careful lifting of stained white reveals
a mass of iridescent black and green,
a purple sac of blood under the closed
fringe of pale lashes, and a cheek like countries
in garish hues on a child's colored map.

"Nothing," she says again, "I fell, that's all."

"Where?"
          "In the hall, outside the bathroom door."
"When?"
          Now the blue Polish eye, unsure,
blinks for a moment. "Not last night; maybe
the night before."
                    "And have you seen a doctor?"

"No! Why? Nothing is wrong with me!" She takes
the flowers and the book of poems, then sits,
abruptly, as if waiting for her guest
to make some further move. Her guarded look,
her stillness under stress, remind the guest
of her friend's past: how she survived Lvov,
when those not blond and blue-eyed disappeared
from city after city; how, escaped
from the slave labor camp, she made her way—
starving, but whole—to write again elsewhere,
learn a new language for what needed saying.

"You know," the guest begins, "you need to stop
picking fights with the neighbors!" And they laugh,
as old friends do over absurdities.

"Well now," the guest says, "shall I water these?"
The hostess shakes her head, with a cold glance
at the straw stems left of her indoor garden,
dangling from powdery dust in crusty pots.
The visitor puts back the pitcher, sits,
wondering what to do. A quiet call
made from the bedroom to the married daughter
living in Jersey; surreptitious searching
to find some doctor's name; the telephone
crammed with unanswered messages, unheard.

The desk is piled with poems—some unfinished—
mingled with bills and still-unopened mail,
and photographs: the son and daughter; infants;
the dead husband, still young, still smiling.
"Where have you sent this sonnet?" asks the guest,
"It's glorious!" Silence, a dazed look;
and then at last, "I don't remember it."

"Are you hungry for lunch?" the guest inquires.
"Of course!" she answers, brightly. "Good! Me too.
What would you like to eat?"
                                        "Nothing," she says,
but slips into her jacket, and replaces
the bandage. Fish and rice, her favorites,
fetched from a nearby restaurant, and then
the daughter—frightened, anxious—at the door,
wary but loving; then the hospital,
whose forms to fill are almost a relief.
Nurses, a gown, a gurney to a room.

After the doctor comes, goodbyes, a promise
to *stay in touch*, and then, before night falls,
the long-awaited visit ends: two buses
through Queens, polyglot streets where ragged shops
announce their wares in foreign alphabets;
the sparkling skyline in the distance; then
two trains: one over roofs and clotheslines, one
under the river, to the city's canyons;
the hotel room downtown, and home tomorrow.

That night, a dream of rowing, effortless,
together, one oar each, on waves of nothing.

Slow-Moving Traffic

Friends in the convoy following your hearse
observe the autumn leaves, agree they've not
quite peaked yet; one mutters a mild curse
when traffic thickens to a blinking clot
of lights around a van with one crushed side.
Through the closed window of a halted car
a stranger stares, as if you were a bride
flaunting your huge bouquet. But where you are,
snug in your creamy satin trimmed with oak,
you are no longer irked by stares, the noise
of sirens, or the whiff of rubbery smoke
that stings the eyes of dressed-up girls and boys.
Impatient at the wheel, your driver's drumming.
In the left lane, somebody's wife is humming.

Resting

But in this grove, in sunny late October,
the dead are much in evidence, in print
that lifts their names and works above the sober
alcoves where they rest, as if by dint
of citing them, stonework announced we mean
to hold them to their contracts. As for ours,
witness the landscape men, alive, who lean
with coils of hose in hand, inscribing showers.
I like the way the dead are made to know
their place—here, where the geese patrol the pond,
with mockingbirds whose clear instructions flow
from leafy towers—and not so far beyond
the labors of the living as to deem
their hours of rest as endless as they seem.

Feet

These feet I'm easing into soft, warm socks
know wilderness and work, war and the street.
Led by these feet, our sons learned rocks,
the pedigree of trees, and the high cost
of everything worth striving for. These feet
marched under banners meant to hold some line:
Hell No, We Won't Go; Desegregate the Schools;
and *No Contract, No Work.*
                                        In '44,
these feet, with those of other green recruits
in Eisenhowers, had learned the winter weather
of the Ardennes, deep in that other war.
Medics would cut away the sodden leather
binding these feet blackening in their boots,
to save them from gangrene.
                                        Many were lost,
but not these: these healed, survived the Rhine
Crossing, and came home to pace among
students learning to arm themselves—with tools.
These feet have walked a lifetime with the young.

When young themselves, these feet, like those of all
children at first, were cradled, safe and small—
see the framed photo—in his mother's hands.

As now in mine, easing them into socks,
hoping to keep them steady when he stands.

Traps

Some every day. The stationery aisle
this morning: someone choosing Christmas cards
nods amiably, calls out, *It's been a while
since I last saw you*, sends you her regards,
and strides off with her cart. I know her face,
but names escape me lately. Anyhow,
why follow her with bad news? Out of place
and out of season, with the whole world now
baited with songs and lights. Traps everywhere:
your basement workshop, where your tools hang, still
ready for use—no safe place even there—
as if death were no obstacle to skill.
Each is at once a blessing and a curse.
And when their ambush ends, that will be worse.

This House

This house is a fallow field
at season's close
where clay and stones are rife,
but nothing grows,

A graveyard of work begun
and tools untended,
since all your joyful labor
abruptly ended.

What breath can reawaken,
what pulse restart,
the beat that once was steady
in its lost heart?

This house is an old instrument
no longer played,
but loud with silent echoes,
music we made.

The Widow Considers Grief

Should this grief abate—
as I'm told it will—
let that happen late,
when I've mourned my fill.

Let no comfort fall
on my lips like rain
until I've paid all
the full toll of pain

levied on our dust
for its first desire,
and pronounced it just,
were it even higher.

The Critic

Regret reads us, trying to decide
what should have been deleted: words unsaid;
words we said wrong, whose echoes, multiplied
by time, play themselves over in a dark
new key; words said that never found their mark
and left a silence there instead.
                                        How clever
regret proves then, revising, bit by bit,
the tone of both the living and the dead,
reworking scene by scene, with here a small
twist to a phrase that gentles its intention,
and there a glance to say the opposite
of words that once made wounds too old to heal.

Regret, in time, attempts outright invention,
speaks over the misspeakings of the real.
And why not? The text is finished, after all,
printed on air, unedited forever.

Portrait

Germany, Schwerte, 1945.
One of the GI buddies he befriended,
a fellow survivor, took this yellowing black-
and-white of my late husband. Still alive!
Grainy vegetation guards his back,
but he's unarmed, taking it easy: done.
He smiles broadly, and squints; does summer sun
blind him, or is it joy? The fighting's ended!
He's healed—though no longer the unhurt
boy who enlisted, or ever again
as deep a sleeper. Not yet twenty-one,
he dreams of girls—we meet six years from then—
and hungers for the honeycake he likes
from mama's kitchen. Outlined in the shirt
pocket of his worn fatigues, a pack
of something I suspect is Lucky Strikes.

The Sharpened Shears He Plied

The sharpened shears he plied
hang useless on the wall,
now that he's gone away,
almost as if they sense—
and mourn—the difference.

The shrubs he used to trim
have swelled, shapeless and dense,
and weeds he kept at bay—
creeper, tendril, and limb—
run rampant through the fence.

But no, tools don't recall
the gardener who died,
and these green things don't care.
No thing remembers him.
How difficult to bear.

After

Of all my images of you, is this—
or that—the one to keep? The sick old man
I washed and fed and diapered like a child,
and eased to sleep with morphine and a kiss;
young, playful father; master artisan;
teacher; author of letters to the press
in which your conscience spoke, unreconciled
to the denial of justice; mandolin-
strummer who chose me for a wife;
soldier home from the front, aged, though still less
than twenty-one, and aching to begin—
given this second chance at life—your life.
You gave yourself to me, with ring and vow.
I kept all of you then. I mean to now.

Album

How jealous of our dead I am these days!
Now that you and I have parted ways
at the last boundary, they've come again
to claim you. Here, the child that you were then,
borne off in sepia on your father's shoulder;
there, at the beach with Sylvia, you seem colder,
beside her long tan legs posed on the sand:
you wave goodbye with an indifferent hand.
In every scene, the dead—as if they knew
you would outlive them—cling to you. And you,
absent everywhere else, seem to have let
yourself be led away, as if some debt
to them outweighed your living vows to me.
But look, I, too, rush toward eternity.

Condolence Call

I saw her—your *Big Blonde*—the other day.
Yes, she dropped in on me, as fantasies
may do, lonely for those who dreamed them up,
and even for the dull realities
like me, who are somehow chosen, preferred,
or settled for.
     I offered her a cup
of coffee and some cookies; what's the harm?
And even sought to lead her by the arm—
as if she had an arm—through souvenirs
you've left me.
     Not the doses of morphine
under your trembling tongue, or now the nights
conversing with your silence. No, I mean
those mutual gifts over our sixty years
and more of sweet and sour together:
work, children, quarrels, losses, pleasure, slights
healed or unhealed by tugging on the tether
that constitutes a marriage.
     But she shook
her non-existent head and backed away,
refused the tour of all my treasures, took
one last look, and left without a word.

How Tiresome

How tiresome, this dying, not at once,
you think, *but incrementally, as year*
by year—or, as of late, every few months:
this spate of thefts by those who leave us here.

A lifelong friend takes half your youth, then some
old dear pilfers the rest, and then your spouse
makes off with all the life there was to come,
till nothing's worth the chores around this house
that you inhabit—that you are. But when
new sprouts throw off the weight of last year's leaves—
February's wreckage—it seems right again
to feed and water them. You know they're thieves,
the young already plotting their goodbye.
Nevertheless you think, *Just one more try.*

How like a Winter . . .

Shakespeare's Sonnet XCVII

So Shakespeare describes *absence*. Yes—but no,
since every winter ends, gentling to spring's
tentative yellows, then the green and blue
and bolder tones of flowering summer. So
has this winter passed, as do all things—
except the final absence. Without you,
for instance, all of time is cut in two—
before and after—seasons all the same,
despite the beckoning lushness of the new,
the living, rich in fur and fins and wings,
intent on resurrection. But they go,
our absent loves, and leave us stranded here,
parted from all the changes of the year
as by an endless fall of pallid snow.

Morning Dreams

You're in my morning dreams routinely now,
busy again, just as you always were:
skimming the *New York Times* with furrowed brow,
snacking, scooping out hommus with a knife
to spread on crackers. And then off you go,
thumping the stairs with those paint-speckled shoes.
I'm trying to catch up, but being you,
you're rushing, with so much still left to do
and no more time. Though I don't think you know—
and just as well—that you've run out of life.
There's nothing to be gained: who needs such news,
with arms at work, their curly golden fur
sprinkled with sawdust and a smear of clay?
What a perfect beginning to the day!

Signing Off

Was there more I meant to say?
Debts to forgive or debts to pay?
Maybe so. But not today.

Errors, I know, I've left behind,
accounts to close or render true,
so much undone I meant to do.

Yes, all of that. But never mind;
I'm leaving it to you, and you.

The Bargain

As if ashamed, Time said, "I'll tell you what:
I can't give anything back, but how about
I teach you how to almost do without
the goods I've repossessed so far? How's that?"

"Well, aren't you all heart," I said. "One hand
makes off with the silverware, and then
the other opens to lend me back again
one plastic teaspoon. I don't understand."

"I'm not such a bad sort," Time said, "you'll see;
but this last offer won't be good forever.
There's so much to reclaim: more bonds to sever,
lights to put out, and speech, and memory.
Trinkets you'll need before I strip you naked.
Do reconsider." And I said, "I'll take it."

RHINA P. ESPAILLAT
HAS PUBLISHED ten full-
length books and three
chapbooks, comprising
poetry, essays, and short
stories, in both English
and her native Spanish,
and translations from
and into both languages.
Her work appears in
many journals, anthologies, and websites, and has earned national
and international awards, including the T. S. Eliot Prize in Poetry, the
Richard Wilbur Award, the Howard Nemerov Prize, the May Sarton
Award, the Robert Frost "Tree at My Window" Prize for translation,
several honors from the New England Poetry Club, the Poetry Society
of America, the Ministry of Culture of the Dominican Republic, and
a Lifetime Achievement Award from Salem State College.

Espaillat's most recent publications are two poetry collection in
English titled *Playing at Stillness* and *Her Place in These Designs*; a
book of Spanish translations titled *Oscura fruta/Dark Berries: Forty-
Two Poems by Richard Wilbur*; and a book of Spanish translations
titled *Algo hay que no es amigo de los muros/Something There Is That
Doesn't Love a Wall: Forty Poems by Robert Frost*.

She is a frequent reader, speaker and workshop leader, and is active
with the Powow River Poets, a literary group she cofounded in 1992.

Also from Able Muse Press

Richard Newman, *All the Wasted Beauty of the World* – Poems

Alfred Nicol, *Animal Psalms* – Poems

Frank Osen, *Virtue, Big as Sin (Able Muse Book Award for Poetry)*

Alexander Pepple (Editor), *Able Muse Anthology;*
Able Muse – a review of poetry, prose & art
(semiannual, winter 2010 on)

James Pollock, *Sailing to Babylon* – Poems

Aaron Poochigian, *The Cosmic Purr* – Poems;
Manhattanite (Able Muse Book Award for Poetry)

Jennifer Reeser, *Indigenous* – Poems

John Ridland, *Sir Gawain and the Green Knight (Anonymous)* – Translation
Pearl (Anonymous) – Translation

Stephen Scaer, *Pumpkin Chucking* – Poems

Hollis Seamon, *Corporeality* – Stories

Ed Shacklee, *The Blind Loon: A Bestiary*

Carrie Shipers, *Cause for Concern (Able Muse Book Award for Poetry)*

Matthew Buckley Smith, *Dirge for an Imaginary World*
(Able Muse Book Award for Poetry)

Barbara Ellen Sorensen, *Compositions of the Dead Playing Flutes* – Poems

Rosemerry Wahtola Trommer, *Naked for Tea* – Poems

Wendy Videlock, *Slingshots and Love Plums* – Poems;
The Dark Gnu and Other Poems;
Nevertheless – Poems

Richard Wakefield, *A Vertical Mile* – Poems

Gail White, *Asperity Street* – Poems

Chelsea Woodard, *Vellum* – Poems

www.ablemusepress.com